Aztecs

Catriona Clarke
Designed by Laura Parker
and Josephine Thompson
Illustrated by Adam Larkum

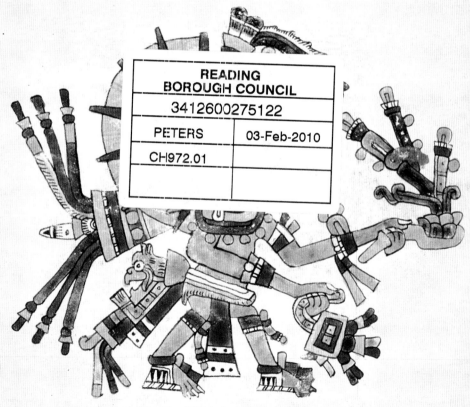

Aztec consultant: Dr. Caroline Dodds, University of Cambridge
Reading consultant: Alison Kelly, Roehampton University

Contents

Who were the Aztecs?

The Aztecs were people who lived in Mexico, until about five hundred years ago.

The Aztecs were very powerful. They ruled over lots of land and people.

This Aztec picture shows some people on a long journey.

Settling down

No one knows exactly where the Aztecs came from. They arrived in Mexico about 700 years ago, looking for a new home.

Other people already lived in all the best places.

After a long journey, they arrived at a lake in a big valley.

They began to build houses on a few islands on the lake.

The Aztecs called their new home Tenochtitlan.

The Aztecs believed that a god had sent a sign telling them where to live.

The sign was an eagle with a snake in its mouth. It was perched on a cactus, as shown in this painting.

Living on the lake

The Aztecs took over lots of land during the next few years. Tenochtitlan grew to become a beautiful city.

The Aztecs built lots of canals so that people could get around by boat.

There were gardens where people grew corn, fruit, flowers and vegetables.

There was a huge square with some temples and a very grand palace.

The palace was so big, there was even a zoo inside.

This old map shows the big square in the middle of the city.

7

The Speaker

The Aztecs were ruled by a very important man. He was known as the Speaker.

No one was allowed to disobey an order from the Speaker.

The Speaker was carried when he went outside. The ground was swept in front of him.

He wore a special costume when he led the Aztecs to war.

8

No one was allowed to turn their back on the Speaker - even when they were walking away from him.

This is an old painting of Montezuma II. He was the last Aztec Speaker.

His shield and cloak are decorated with feathers.

what to wear

There were strict rules about what people were allowed to wear.

Only rich nobles were allowed to wear bright, patterned clothes.

Ordinary Aztecs wore plain clothes that were made out of rough material.

Priests dressed in black and never washed their long, tangled hair.

This picture of a warrior is from an Aztec book.

The best warriors were allowed to wear clothes with lots of feathers and decoration.

Any warrior who captured four prisoners became very important.

Everyday life

Lots of people lived in houses next to a canal.

The white walls kept the houses cool in the hot sun.

Everyone slept on mats on the floor inside their house.

Most food was cooked inside on a small fire.

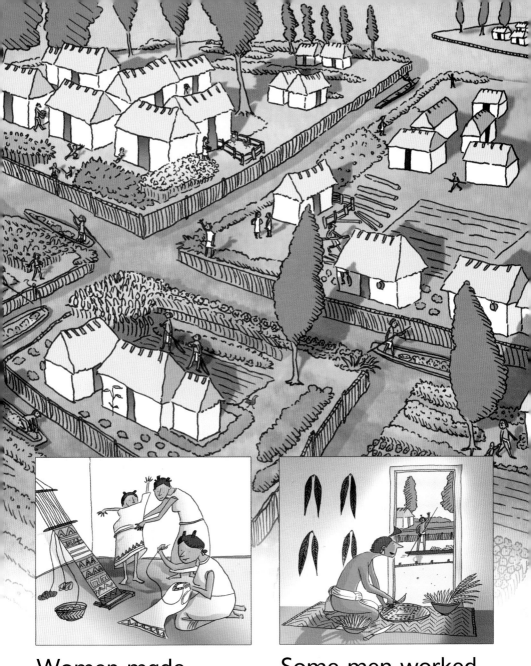

Women made clothes for their families to wear.

Some men worked at home, making things to sell.

13

Growing up

Children were very important to the Aztecs. They had to behave well. Very naughty children were punished.

This boy is being held over a fire with chillies burning in it.

The smoke would sting his eyes.

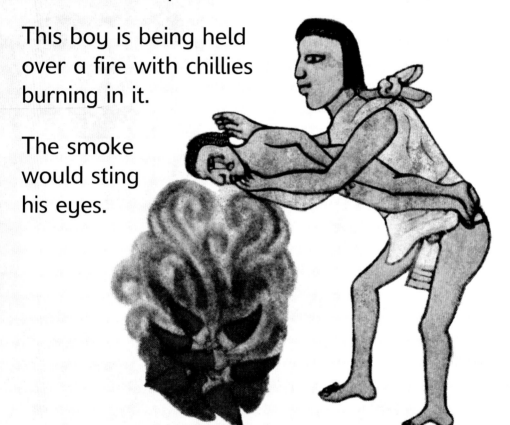

Baby boys were given a tiny bow and arrow when they were born.

Young children had
to help their parents
with jobs like fishing.

At school, girls and
boys learned to
sing and dance.

Some boys went to
a special school to
train to be priests.

Food and drink

The Aztecs ate lots of vegetables and beans, but not much meat. They liked spicy food.

Jars like these were used to store food.

They were often decorated with animals.

The Aztecs liked to wrap all kinds of food in tortillas.

To make tortillas, they ground corn on a stone to make flour.

Then, they added water to the flour to make a dough.

The dough was made into tortillas which were cooked.

The Aztecs loved to drink chocolate - they added chillies to make it spicy!

Buying and selling

There was a busy market near the city. People went there to buy and swap things.

More than 50,000 people visited the market every day.

Some stalls sold fruit and flowers, and some sold live animals such as turkeys and dogs.

There were precious stones for sale, and animal skins too.

The Aztecs didn't have money - they sometimes used cocoa beans to buy things instead.

The ball game

The Aztecs played a very exciting game called tlachtli. There were two teams.

The players wore padding to protect themselves from the hard rubber ball.

They could only hit the ball with their hips, knees and elbows. This could hurt a lot.

The players tried to get the ball through the stone ring high on the wall.

This is a goal ring. It was
very hard to score a goal,
because the hole was so small.

The winners could take
any belongings they
liked from the crowd.

Gods and goddesses

The Aztecs believed in lots of different gods and goddesses. They held lots of festivals to worship them.

This is a mask of a very powerful god called Feathered Snake.

It is made from lots of tiny pieces of a stone called turquoise.

The god of sun and war was called Hummingbird on the Left.

Hummingbird on the Left's mother was an earth goddess called Snake Skirt.

The Aztecs believed that the god of water brought rain, thunder and lightning.

Smoking Mirror was god of the night sky. He decided if people would be lucky.

Giving blood

The Aztecs believed that their gods had to be fed with human hearts and blood.

Priests killed prisoners at the top of a temple. This is called human sacrifice.

People thought this was a good way to die because it helped the gods.

More than 10,000 people were once sacrificed in just four days.

Sometimes a strong enemy prisoner was given weapons and tied to a round stone.

He fought the best Aztec warriors. The fight ended when the prisoner was badly injured.

The priests cut out the prisoner's heart and offered it to the gods.

In battle

The Aztecs often went to war to capture people for human sacrifice.

Every man in the city got ready to go off to fight when they heard the war drum.

The best warriors were eagle knights and jaguar knights. They wore special clothes.

The warriors usually didn't try to kill the enemy - they took them prisoner instead.

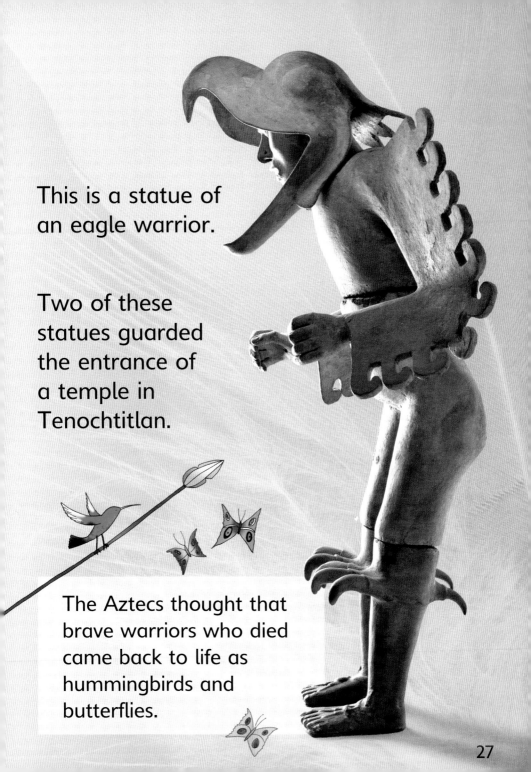

This is a statue of an eagle warrior.

Two of these statues guarded the entrance of a temple in Tenochtitlan.

The Aztecs thought that brave warriors who died came back to life as hummingbirds and butterflies.

Under attack!

In 1519, Spanish soldiers arrived in Tenochtitlan. They had sailed across the ocean seaching for treasure.

When they arrived, the Aztecs welcomed them. But the Spanish were shocked when they saw that the Aztecs sacrificed people.

The Spanish wanted to take over the city, so they attacked it. In 1521, they captured the city and killed lots of people.

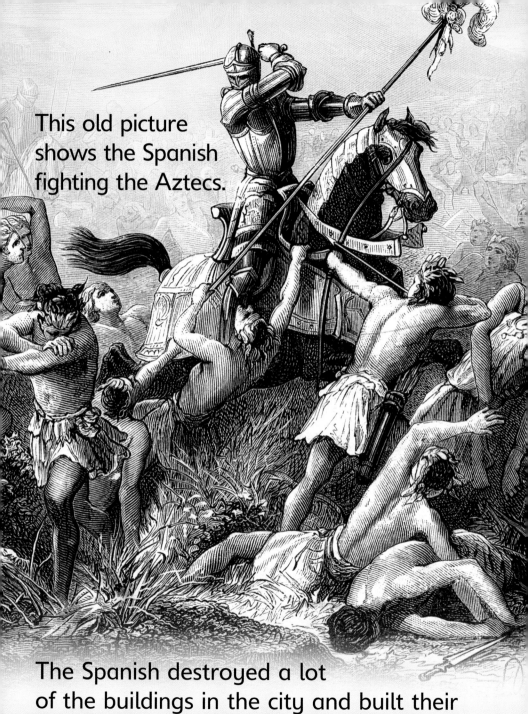

This old picture
shows the Spanish
fighting the Aztecs.

The Spanish destroyed a lot
of the buildings in the city and built their
own. This was the end of the Aztec era.

Glossary of Aztec words

Here are some of the words in this book you might not know. This page tells you what they mean.

 noble - a rich Aztec. Nobles wore nice clothes and precious jewels.

 Speaker - the ruler of the Aztecs. He lived in a huge palace.

 chillies - seed pods from pepper plants. Chillies make food taste hot.

 tortilla - say 'tor-tee-yah'. A pancake made from flour and water.

 cocoa beans - seeds that can be used to make chocolate.

 tlachtli - say 'tul-act-lee'. A ball game played by the Aztecs.

 sacrifice - a gift for the gods. The Aztecs made human sacrifices.

Websites to visit

If you have a computer, you can find out more about the Aztecs on the Internet. On the Usborne Quicklinks Website there are links to four fun websites.

Website 1 - Look at a 3-D model of Tenochtitlan.

Website 2 - Listen to an Aztec song.

Website 3 - Help a tlachtli player get ready for a ball game.

Website 4 - See an Aztec sculpture of a jaguar.

To visit these websites, go to **www.usborne-quicklinks.com** Read the Internet safety guidelines, and then type the keywords "beginners aztecs".

The websites are regularly reviewed and the links in Usborne Quicklinks are updated. However, Usborne Publishing is not responsible, and does not accept liability, for the content or availability of any website other than its own. We recommend that children are supervised while on the Internet.

This stone knife is decorated with a face. It was used for human sacrifices.

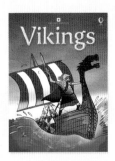

Vikings

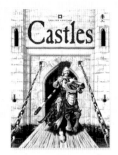

Castles

How flowers grow

Knights

Living in space

Caterpillars and Butterflies

Ballet

Pirates

Egyptians

Eggs and Chicks

Romans

Dinosaurs

Tadpoles and frogs

Why do we eat?

Under the sea

Weather